BEDSIDE PRAYERS

Also by June Cotner

GRACES: PRAYERS & POEMS FOR EVERYDAY
MEALS AND SPECIAL OCCASIONS

THE HOME DESIGN HANDBOOK:
THE ESSENTIAL PLANNING GUIDE FOR BUILDING,
BUYING, OR REMODELING A HOME

BEDSIDE
PRAYERS

PRAYERS & POEMS
FOR WHEN YOU RISE
AND GO TO SLEEP

JUNE COTNER

HarperLargePrint
A Division of HarperCollinsPublishers

A hardcover edition of this book was pulished in 1997 by HarperSan Francisco, a division of HarperCollinsPublishers, Inc.

Permissions and acknowledgments appear on page 159 and constitute a continuation of this copyright page.

First large print edition published 1999.

The Library of Congress has catalogued the hardcover edition as follows:
Bedside prayers : prayers and poems for when you rise and go to sleep / [selected by] June Cotner.
    Includes bibliographical references.
    ISBN 0-06-251529-2 (cloth)
      1. Religious poetry, American. 2. Spiritual life—Poetry.
3. Prayers. I. Cotner, June.
PS595.R4B37 1997
811.008'0382—dc21   97-19818
ISBN 0-06-093319-4
99 00 01 02 03 ❖ RRD(H) 10 9 8 7 6 5 4 3 2 1

This book is dedicated to
my husband, Jim Graves,
my sister, Sue Cotner,
and my uncle, Bill Cotner—
who have all given me
love, comfort, and inspiration.

CONTENTS

Two **COMFORT**

Four **NIGHTFALL**

Five **MORNING**

THANKS

Bedside Prayers would not have been written without an inquiry from my editor at HarperSanFrancisco, Lisa Bach, asking, "Would you be interested in doing a book about prayers and poems to rise and sleep by?" The suggestion delighted me immensely. I love to read spiritual poetry in the comfort of my bed, whether upon arising on a lazy Saturday or Sunday, or after a long day. Surely, I thought, there would be others like me.

In choosing sample selections for the *Bedside Prayers* proposal, I combed through countless anthologies seeking spiritual prayers and poems that would speak to one's heart and soul, offering comfort during troubled times and inspiration during good times. Throughout this process, my agent, Denise Marcil, gave me excellent feedback and encouragement. After she sold the book to HarperSanFrancisco, *The Writer* ran a call for submissions in their November *1996* issue. In addition, I placed advertisements in poetry magazines. Overall, I received more than three thousand submissions.

My husband, high school sweetheart, and faithful soulmate, Jim Graves, helped me select poems that most readers, both male and female, would enjoy. We read many of the poems aloud to each other, and Jim offered the male perspective as well as an additional sounding board for the rhythm, flow, and meaning of the various pieces.

When all the selections that felt good to me were gathered, twenty copies of the 250-page manuscript were prepared to be critiqued by friends, relatives, and professional colleagues, ranging in age from seventeen to eighty-seven. I purposely selected individuals who represented a wide range of religious and spiritual beliefs to help select the final content of the book.

Two individuals, Patty Henderson and Maribeth Gibbons, who each had purchased four copies of my previous book, *Graces*, (even prior to meeting me!) willingly agreed to critique *Bedside Prayers*.

Also, I'd like to thank my sister, Sue Cotner; my son, Kyle Myrvang; and my daughter, Kirsten Cotner Myrvang, for rating the selections. Special appreciation goes to the following dear friends and manuscript critiquers: Arnie Anfinson, Stephanie Brochier, Patty Forbes Cheng, Sue Gitch, Fern Halgren, Patricia Huckell, Susan Peterson, Lynn Eathorne Pulliam, and Sandra Van Ausdal.

Jo Ann Haun, the editor of my first book, *The Home Design Handbook*, now an independent book editor in New York City, kindly agreed to offer me feedback on the manuscript. When I was promoting *Graces*, I was fortunate to cross paths with Father Paul Keenan, host of "Religion on the Line" and "As You Think" and author of *Good News for Bad Days*. He enthusiastically agreed to critique *Bedside Prayers*.

And how good can a book of spiritual poetry be without making sure that poets give their professional nod of approval? Deepest gratitude goes to the following poets for lending their considerable expertise: Barbara Crooker (winner of many poetry awards), Penny Harter (author of *Turtle Blessing* and thirteen other books), Arlene Gay Levine (author of *39 Ways to Open Your Heart*), and Mary A. Summerline (who has been published in numerous anthologies and magazines).

I would also like to thank Lillie Malone for steering me to "Beatitudes for Friends of the Aged," Teri Waag for kindly slipping me a copy of "The Grace of God" when she sensed I needed the comfort of those words, Jamie Isgar for showing me "Cheer Up, My Soul!" from one of his antique poetry books, Kevin Jennings for keeping my computer cooperative, Suzanne Long for lengthy stretches of word processing with good cheer, Shawna Sitton for proofreading the manuscript on short notice, and a very understanding boss, George B. Wittler, who gave me some time off from my position at the Poulsbo office of The Onyx Group, an architectural and planning firm, to complete the book.

My heartfelt gratitude goes out to the contributors themselves, who provided the outstanding poems that shape the heart and soul of *Bedside Prayers*. Although I lived and breathed *Bedside Prayers* for months without a break, my reward is the pleasure in creating a poetic symphony for so many of your wonderful voices to be heard.

And without you, God, this book would not be possible. We are the hearts and souls and voices that reach our highest selves to You.

A LETTER TO READERS

I hope *Bedside Prayers* will give you the comfort of a warm blanket, the inspiration of a shooting star, and reflections for living life well.

The book is divided into five sections. I envision readers will turn to the "Inspiration" chapter when life is going well and they have energy to give to others. The "Comfort" chapter will offer solace during times of disappointment, sadness, and setbacks. A person in a peaceful, contemplative frame of mind might turn to the "Reflections" section. The "Nightfall" chapter should provide the perfect sleep enticement. And the "Morning" chapter will give good and inspiring thoughts on carrying through the day—and offer ideas on how we can kindly give back to others.

I believe poetry offers the highest, most creative expression of humankind. Most of us are too busy these days to read a book on self-improvement or an essay on "doing good." But a short poem that captures the essence of ten self-improvement books will lift anyone's spirit!

The idea of finding poems that express the thoughts contained in an entire book or often an entire experience intrigues me. I want to continue creating these kinds of spiritual anthologies. I enjoy finding the nugget that expresses the soul of an idea. The enduring anthologies contain poems that speak to the emotions we all experience, not just to the specific experience of one individual.

My upcoming anthologies are listed on pages 153 and 154. If you would like to contribute a spiritual poem to a future anthology or you come across a poem you think I would enjoy, please send it to:

June Cotner
P.O. Box 2765
Poulsbo, WA 98370

Inspiration

PART ONE

IN ALL ENDEAVORS

In all endeavors
Strive to celebrate
The spirit of the warrior . . .
Calm,
Centered,
Certain . . .
Whether tending to the flower garden
Or searching for the heart of
   the divine.

JO-ANNE ROWLEY

THESE ARE THE GIFTS I ASK

These are the gifts I ask
Of Thee, Spirit serene:
Strength for the daily task,
Courage to face the road,
Good cheer to help me bear the
traveler's load,
And, for the hours of rest that
come between,
An inward joy of all things heard
and seen.

HENRY VAN DYKE

THE CANDLE

Put a candle in your window
When the night is dark with storm.
It will welcome any stranger;
Keep friends and family warm.

When you see someone in sorrow;
Just let your candle shine
From your soul and from your window
It will be a cheerful sign.

Always place a candle
Where the world can see its light—
The glow will lift a sad heart
And brighten every night.

JOAN STEPHEN

ILLUMINATION

It is better to light candles
than to curse the darkness.
It is better to plant seeds
than to accuse the earth.
The world needs all of our power
and love and energy,
and each of us has something that
we can give.
The trick is to find it and use it,
to find it and give it away.
So there will always be more.
We can be lights for each other,
and through each other's
illumination
we will see the way.
Each of us is a seed,
a silent promise,
and it is always spring.

MERLE SHAIN

THE GIFT

The gift of encouragement
Should be given each day—
Pass it out freely
And in gentle ways.
There's no need for ribbons
To make it look grand—
Just the simple encouragement
Of a kind, helping hand.

JOAN STEPHEN

LET ME BE A LIGHT

Let me be a light, O God,
That shines for all to see;
If someone needs to find the way,
An example may I be
Of love and kindness and brotherhood,
Of all that's gentle, of all that's good.

THERESA MARY GRASS

THESE I WISH

To live a life of cheer
  To laugh when all seems dark
  To shed a tender tear
    When beauty calls, to hark!

To speak a word of hope
  To love, to work, to pray
  To bring a touch of joy
    To all I meet each day.

I would be glad, glad, GLAD!
  And live with all my heart
  That when I come to die
    I may have left my part.

MONICA MILLER

GIVE ME A KIND HEART

Give me a kind heart that will endure,
One that's strong and secure.
To help someone along the way,
May this be my goal every day.
Let me lend a helping hand
To someone whose life has not gone
as planned,
Reaching out to one in need,
May this be my daily good deed,
To provide a guiding light
For someone lost in the dark of night.
Let me take time to care
For someone experiencing despair.

Whatever I do, everywhere I go,
Your Will, Dear Lord, let me know.

EVE KILEY

POET'S PRAYER

In You through whom
all things speak,
use me please
to sing your song.

KATE ROBINSON

PLEASE HELP ME WASH MY DAYS

O God, please help me wash my days
And hang them on the line to dry.
Please help me scrub my months
And shake them out,
Soak my years,
And dry them in the summer sun.
Please help me wear a suit
Of honest fabric, clean and plain.

YAACOR DAVID SHULMAN

HEART OF MY HEART

While striding on life's pathway
fill up your days with cheer
just laugh at rainbows, small or great,
to banish every fear.

Hold tight to what life offers
content with all you do
for all adventures help create
the treasure that is you.

KRIS EDIGER

TO BE STILL

Focus my speech
within the light
that all my words
be holy, bright.
   Hold my mind
   within your hand
   that all my thoughts
   be your command.
Still my heart
within your gift
that every choice
be inspired, swift.
   Center my life
   within your heart
   that every act
   reflects your art.

JOANNA M. WESTON

SUCCESS

To laugh often and much;
to win the respect of intelligent people
and the affection of children;
to earn the appreciation of honest
critics
and to endure the betrayal of false
friends;
to appreciate beauty;
to find the best in others;
to leave the world a bit better,
whether by a healthy child,
a garden path
or a redeemed social condition;
to know even one life
has breathed easier
because you have lived.
This is to have succeeded.

RALPH WALDO EMERSON

WINGS

Oh, to catch the winds of flight
And soar where eagles go,
To leave the woes of troubled souls
Behind me far below.
I'd listen to the song of birds
And sail in endless flight,
Then chase the sun through cloudy paths
And play with stars at night.

The boundless heavens for my home,
The breeze to lift me high,
To rise above my mortal bonds
And never have to die.
Knowing I had found the way
To trails where angels trod,
And when my wings could fly no more—
I'd take the hand of GOD!

C. DAVID HAY

HOLD FAST YOUR DREAMS

Hold fast your dreams!
Within your heart
Keep one still, secret spot
Where dreams may go,
And, sheltered so,
May thrive and grow
Where doubt and fear are not.
O keep a place apart,
Within your heart,
For little dreams to go!

LOUISE DRISCOLL

THE VOICE WITHIN

I took a little walk today
To listen to God's word,
And when I stopped to rest awhile
This is what I heard:

"Dear one, there's someone waiting
To hear from you today,
Someone who needs your loving heart
To spread joy in its own way;
Never turn away my child
I bid you to press on.
Let your light forever shine
To reach this precious one.
Who knows what happiness can come
From loving thoughts so true,
Go forth and spread your sunshine
Only good can come to you."

And as I left my quiet place
I felt such peace within,
Because I knew what I should do
To love and honor Him.

JAN EDWARDS

THE INNER FLAME

I am not more than
a wisp
    of
    smoke
to the world,
but
to God
I am a flame of hope and promise
in a darkened room.

JOAN NOËLDECHEN

MAKING LIFE WORTHWHILE

May every soul that touches mine—
Be it the slightest contact—
Get therefrom some good;
Some little grace; one kindly thought;
One aspiration yet unfelt;
One bit of courage
For the darkening sky;
One gleam of faith
To brave the thickening ills of life;
One glimpse of brighter skies
Beyond the gathering mists—
To make this life worthwhile
And heaven a surer heritage.

GEORGE ELIOT

ALIVE

The most visible creators I know of
are those artists whose medium
is life itself.

The ones who express
the inexpressible—
without brush, hammer, clay, or
guitar.
They neither paint nor sculpt—
their medium is being.

Whatever their presence touches
has increased life.
They see and don't have to draw.
They are the artists of being
alive.

J. STONE

DO ALL THE GOOD YOU CAN

Do all the good you can,
By all the means you can,
In all the ways you can,
In all the places you can,
At all the times you can,
To all the people you can,
As long as ever you can.

JOHN WESLEY

COMFORT

PART TWO

DAILY PRAYER

From the sun's early rising
into the night
Bless us, O Lord,
with your guiding light.

And then through the dark
to dawn's golden flare,
Watch over us, Lord,
keep us in your care.

THERESA MARY GRASS

HEAVEN, BLOW THROUGH ME

Heaven, blow through me.
Lift me past edges of my life.
Cast me in a clearer light.
Scoop me up trembling, spent.
Certain I have nothing left to give.
Give me comfort, solace,
blood flowing through my heart.
That I breathe Your breath
at last.

MEG CAMPBELL

TRIFLE

Against the day of the sorrow
Lay by some trifling thing
A smile, a kiss, a flower
For sweet remembering.

Then when the day is darkest
Without one rift of blue
Take out your little trifle
And dream your dream anew.

GEORGIA DOUGLAS JOHNSON

HOPE

Hope is the thing with feathers
That perches on the soul,
And sings the tune without the words,
And never stops at all,

And sweetest in the gale is heard;
And sore must be the storm
That could abash the little bird
That kept so many warm.

I've heard it in the chillest land,
And on the strangest sea;
Yet, never, in extremity,
It asked a crumb of me.

EMILY DICKINSON

THE COMFORTER

I fought the tears and ran outside
From human eye I'd try to hide
But there are Eyes that always see
He ever watches over me
And so He sent a gentle breeze
to kiss my cheek and comfort me.

EMILY KING

THE TEST

Oh, yes, I've reached those golden days
You hear so much about;
I don't feel any older yet,
But will one day, no doubt.

The sky is still a lovely blue,
The rose is just as sweet.
Each day is like another chance
To make my life complete.

Sure, there's hardship, sorrow and pain,
Who thought there wouldn't be?
But now I know it's just a test
To find the worth in me.

BETTY IREAN LOEB

THE THING IS

The thing is
to love life
to love it even when you have no
stomach for it, when everything you've
   held
dear crumbles like burnt paper in your
   hands
and your throat is filled with the silt of it.
When grief sits with you so heavily
it is like heat, tropical, moist
thickening the air so it's heavy like water
more fit for gills than lungs.
When grief weights you like your own
   flesh
only more of it, an obesity of grief.
How long can a body withstand this, you
   think,
and yet you hold life like a face between
   your palms,
a plain face, with no charming smile
or twinkle in her eye,
and you say, yes, I will take you
I will love you, again.

ELLEN BASS

SOMEHOW

Life's struggle
can be puzzling now & then.

Somehow
at the most difficult times
we find wings to fly.

CORRINE DeWINTER

CHEER UP, MY SOUL!

Cheer up, my soul!
faith's moonbeams softly glisten
Upon the breast of life's most
troubled sea;
And it will cheer
thy drooping heart to listen
To those brave songs which angels
mean for thee.

FREDERICK WILLIAM FABER
(1814–1863)
Pilgrims of the Night

ENCLOSED IN WONDER

God of the Wind,
    Spirit God,
You, God, Larger than Life,
    Greater than the Day,
        Fuller than the Event,
I can be alone with You.
        Alone with the Alone.
I feel scattered.
    Yet centered, breathing,
        Allowing your spirit to be in my
    sensing.
    I dance and settle and move on.
    Slowly.
        Present to the Moment,
Full of human frailty and longing,
Enclosed in joy and wonder.

DONNA J. MAEBORI

TRUST HIM

During sad troubles
Or times of distress
Earnestly praying
Will lessen the stress.

When there is sorrow
Or the future seems dim;
Pause for a moment
And put trust in Him.

JOAN STEPHEN

WHO YOU ARE

You are a rare wild orchid, magically lit
  from within,
but warmed outside by flaming sun of
  passion.
You are strong, and cling tenaciously to
  love.
No jungle predator can tear you from your
  home,
for you protect your own.
But when shrieking storms have blown
  down
all the stable trunks of home,
and you stand swaying in the shifting wind,
know this, my friend:
You are more than who you think.
No one can define you, or diminish you,
even at the brink of loss and sorrow.
You fold within yourself
seeds of growth and power,
the light of understanding.
These contain the blueprint of your larger
  family.

WAVE CARBERRY

PSALM OF TRANQUILITY

Everything that's needed
Is given us each day;
Reflected in still waters
And grasses by the way.

Our souls are guided daily
By an unseen welcome hand;
Leading ever onward
To some sweet peaceful land.

There is no fear of evil
Or death or shades of gloom.
Constant is our comfort
Even beyond the tomb.

Goodness will always follow;
Forever and a day
So all may live in paradise
With no need to repay.

JOAN STEPHEN

PERSPECTIVE

In the loneliest moments there are
bugs in the wilderness
charming, industrious
with precise, dainty feet
and long, sensitive feelers.

JUDY KLASS

A LOVE THAT NEVER FAILS

There is an eye that never sleeps
Beneath the wing of night;
There is an ear that never shuts
When sinks the beams of light.
There is an arm that never tires
When human strength gives way;
There is a love that never fails
When earthly love decays.

GEORGE MATHESON

A PRIVATE PLACE

Give me a private place, oh God
Where I can turn to thee,
Grant me the blessed solitude
To pray for what need be.
Help me to do a golden deed
For all my fellow men,
Plant within me kindness
From day's beginning till its end.

Show me wherein each path to take
To lift some weary load,
Make me understand thereafter
I will have reaped what I have sowed.
Let me soothe a breaking heart
Or chase away a tear,
Oh God, if I can only do my part,
Peace will come to me.

JAN EDWARDS

LIFE'S LESSONS

I learn, as the years roll onward
  And leave the past behind,
That much I had counted sorrow
  But proves that God is kind;
That many a flower I had longed for
  Had hidden a thorn of pain,
And many a rugged bypath
  Led to fields of ripened grain.

The clouds that cover sunshine
  They cannot banish the sun;
And the earth shines out the brighter
  When the weary rain is done.
We must stand in the deepest shadow
  To see the clearest light;
And often through wrong's own
  darkness
  Comes the very strength of light.

AUTHOR UNKNOWN

SERENITY PRAYER

God grant me the serenity
to accept the things I cannot change,
Courage to change the things I can,
and wisdom to know the difference.
Amen.

REINHOLD NIEBUHR

LORD OF LIFE

Lord of Life, guide my hand
Reveal to me thy master plan
Of all things I could do and say
to bring to life thy Will today

Lord of Life, open my heart
Instruct me in the simple art
of going within this sacred space
to hear your Word, receive your Grace

Lord of Life, support my soul
when times of tests and pain unfold
Remind me then, I've chosen this:
a way to grow, the road to bliss

Lord of Life, surround my being
with tender light of timeless healing
So love on every side abounds
from me to others and back around

Lord of Life, I humbly thank thee
for all the beauty around and in me
Flower, snow, wind and tree
Your blessings are everywhere
endless and free.

ARLENE GAY LEVINE

VOICE IN MY SILENCE

I believe that God is in me
as the sun is in the color and fragrance
of a flower—
the Light in my darkness,
the Voice in my silence.

HELEN KELLER

(Helen Keller became blind and deaf
in infancy and never experienced
the reality of human speech.)

OUR RIDE AMONG THE STARS

FOR WILLIAM STAFFORD

Divine One
We live and breathe
Your great goodness.
Bless us
With your healing spirit.

Let It rest among us,
So that we may see
With restored vision
Ourselves,
The gift of life,
And our ride among the stars.

SHIRLEY KOBAR

WHATEVER IS—IS BEST

I know, as my life grows older,
    And mine eyes have clearer sight,
That under each rank wrong some-
    where
        There lies the root of Right;

That each sorrow has its purpose,
    By the sorrowing oft unguessed;
But as sure as the sun brings morning,
    Whatever is—is best.

I know that each sinful action,
    As sure as the night brings shade,
Is somewhere, sometime punished,
    Tho' the hour be long delayed.
I know that the soul is aided
    Sometimes by the heart's unrest,
And to grow means often to suffer—
    But whatever is—is best.

I know there are no errors,
   In the great Eternal plan,

And all things work together
   For the final good of man.

And I know when my soul speeds onward,
   In its grand Eternal quest,
I shall say as I look back earthward,
   Whatever is—is best.

ELLA WHEELER WILCOX

RIVER AND SKY

Move our hearts with the calm,
smooth flow of your grace.
Let the river of your love
run through our souls.
May my soul be carried
by the current of your love,
towards the wide, infinite ocean
    of heaven.

Stretch out my heart with your
    strength,
as you stretch out the sky above the
    earth.
Smooth out any wrinkles of hatred
    or resentment.
Enlarge my soul that it may know
    more fully your truth.

GILBERT OF HOYLAND
DIED C.1170

THE SHIP OF LIFE

Steer the ship of my life, good Lord,
to your quiet harbor,
where I can be safe from the storms
of sin and conflict.
Show me the course I should take.
Renew in me the gift of discernment,
so that I can always see the right
direction in which I should go.
And give me the strength and the
courage
to choose the right course,
even when the sea is rough
and the waves are high,
knowing that through enduring
hardship and danger in your name
we shall find comfort and peace.

BASIL OF CAESAREA
c.330–379

LORD, HELP ME

Lord, help me to persist although I
  want to give up.
Lord, help me to keep trying although
  I can't see what good it does.
Lord, help me to keep praying al-
  though I'm not sure You hear me,
Lord, help me to keep living in ways
  that seek to please You.

Lord, help me to know when to lead
  and when to follow.
Lord, help me to know when to speak
  and when to remain silent.
Lord, help me to know when to act and
  when to wait.

MARIAN WRIGHT EDELMAN

A PRAYER FOR TRUE UNDERSTANDING

O God
Give me understanding
Teach me patience and acceptance.
Whatever happened in the past,
   happened for the best.
Whatever is happening now, is also
   happeningfor the best.
I came with nothing and I will leave
   with nothing.
What belonged to someone else
   yesterday is mine today,
What is mine today will belong
   to someone else tomorrow.
In this ever-changing world
Is an unchanging principle
Which is within my own being.
Contentment and freedom arise from
   true understanding
The Self is one and the same in all.

SWAMI NITAYANANDA
INDIA, TWENTIETH CENTURY

THE LAND OF ETERNAL LOVE

Though I am bewildered by troubles,
   And feel I can no longer cope,
Somewhere out in the darkness
   There exists a ray of hope;
A lamp that will light my pathway,
   A gift from God above,
A light that will guide my footsteps
   To the Land of Eternal Love.

It's a land of peace and contentment,
   Where the power of God transcends;
A place where strangers are welcomed,
   Where neighbors are always friends.
It's a place that has no evil,
   And no need for locks on doors.
It's a land of unspoiled beauty,
   Free of the ravages of wars.

It's a land that will know no sickness,
    Where the lame will be made whole;
Where pain will cause no sorrow,
    And death will take no toll.
It's a place where sins are forgiven
    By Him who reigns above.
I hope someday to go there,
    To the Land of Eternal Love.

MARY A. SUMMERLINE

THE GRACE OF GOD

The Will of God
can never lead you
where the grace of God
cannot keep you.

AUTHOR UNKNOWN

REFLECTIONS

PART THREE

WHISPERS AT THE ALTAR

Let there be a window in my knowing;
That I might bend, unfolding as a bright
  stem to light

Keep me fluid in my certainties;
That I might shape myself to each
  seamless vessel
As the sea to the shoulders of the earth

Let expectation be a loose garment;
That I might wear my disappointments
As a changing wind, its clouds

Add to my ambition a wide heaven;
That when doubt and failure like
  fluttering birds
Cast shadows,
I might wait for wisdom with patient
  branches

Keep hidden from me all that I might
  understand;
That when I search the vast darkness,
Stars may keep their wonder

Hold me steadfast in my unfulfillment;
For to hear love, only the yearning heart
May listen

MARILYN SHELTON

I LIVE MY LIFE IN WIDENING CIRCLES

I live my life in widening circles
that reach out across the world.
I may not ever complete the last one,
but I give myself to it.

I circle around God, that primordial tower.
I have been circling for thousands of years,
and I still don't know: am I a falcon,
a storm, or a great song?

RAINER MARIA RILKE
Rilke's Book of Hours: Love Poems to God
TRANSLATED BY ANITA BARROWS AND JOANNA
MACY

AM I SO VAIN TO THINK THESE THOUGHTS ARE MINE?

Angels
immortal, guardian
shouting, fluttering, trumpeting
we hear only whispers
ideas

JOAN E. SHROYER-KENO

EPIPHANY

It was Einstein who said
either nothing is a miracle,
or everything is—
a jagged mountain range,
lilacs in bloom,
a peacock unfurled,
sun on your arm,
the touch of a stranger.

Take your pick: be surprised
by nothing at all,
or by everything that is.

MARYANNE HANNAN

THINGS I NEED TO KNOW

How can we love this world?
Where do people hide their feelings?
Why is the cerulean of sky a healing?
When do you understand your soul
is the only gold you'll ever own?
Who can say, without fear, they are unique
yet one with everyone?
Will you open your heart?
Is there time?
Does anything else matter?

ARLENE GAY LEVINE

YOU SEE, I WANT A LOT

You see, I want a lot.
Maybe I want it all:
the darkness of each endless fall,
the shimmering light of each ascent.

So many are alive who don't seem to
    care.
Casual, easy, they move in the world
as though untouched.

But you take pleasure in the faces
of those who know they thirst.
You cherish those
who grip you for survival.

You are not dead yet, it's not too late
to open your depths by plunging into
    them
and drink in the life
that reveals itself quietly there.

RAINER MARIA RILKE
Rilke's Book of Hours: Love Poems to God
TRANSLATED BY ANITA BARROWS AND
JOANNA MACY

SOUL-HOME

Where does the spirit live?
  Inside or outside
Things remembered, made things,
  things unmade?

—SEAMUS HEANEY

The soul's home is not the body—
the body craves and decays.
And the soul's home is not
a church, a house, a room—
they hold only empty space.
The soul-home is a tone,
vibrations of emotion
sustained.

A poem can house a soul—so can
a painting or a song. And
a soul will sing on invisible
strings, on resonant chords
of a love that simply
accompanies.

GALE SWIONTKOWSKI

NOT A SPOON, A KEY

We open memories
like Hershey's cocoa—
the lid sticks tight.

We think the past
has happened,
is fixed as a photograph
locked in an album,
but it changes, it develops,
mixed with time,
like sugar mixes in
that dark and bitter powder,
making a drink
that warms and restores.

BARBARA CROOKER

LIFE IS LOVE AND LOVE IS LIVING

Feeling strong and strongly feeling.
Being glad and glad of being.
Care for need and needing caring.
Sharing self and selfless sharing.
Full of spirit spirit filling.
Will is warm and warmly willing.
Giving joy enjoy the giving.
Life is love and love is living.

JOSEPH BYRON

MOST RICHLY BLESSED
(PRAYER OF AN UNKNOWN CONFEDERATE SOLDIER)

I asked God for strength, that I might
    achieve,
I was made weak, that I might learn
    humbly to obey . . .
I asked for health, that I might do
    greater things,
I was given infirmity, that I might do
    better things . . .
I asked for riches, that I might be happy,
I was given poverty, that I might be wise . . .
I asked for power, that I might have the
    praise of men,
I was given weakness, that I might feel
    the need of God . . .
I asked for all things, that I might
    enjoy life,
I was given life, that I might enjoy
    all things . . .
I got nothing that I asked for—but
    everything that I had hoped for.
Almost despite myself, my unspoiled
    prayers were answered.
I am among all men, most richly blessed.

AUTHOR UNKNOWN

WHAT WAS HIS CREED?

What was his creed?
I do not know his creed, I only know
That here below, he walked the
    common road
And lifted many a load, lightened
    the task,
Brightened the day for others toiling
    on a weary way:
This, his only meed; I do not know
    his creed.

His creed? I care not what his creed;
Enough that never yielded he to greed,
But served a brother in his daily need;
Plucked many a thorn and planted
    many a flower;
Glorified the service of each hour;
Had faith in God, himself, and
    fellow-men;—
Perchance he never thought in terms
    of creed,
I only know he lived a life, in deed!

 H. N. FIFER

A MIDNIGHT CONVERSATION
WITH GOD

God, why is it
that the only time
I swim back to You
is when the sharks
are about to eat me?
I could harbor my soul
in your crystal, clean waters
but instead
I allow the undertow
to carry me far from You
and out into
the black, salty waters
where danger lurks
with each crashing wave
and where my feet
never touch the bottom.

MIKE W. BLOTTENBERGER

A MIRACLE

It's a miracle how the Bed
nestles us safely
a third of our lives
as the eight-thousand-mile-thick earth
beneath us twirls, pulling
the atmosphere around itself
like a whirling shawl.

Somehow we wake up
not at all dizzy, slide out,
feet on the floor, stand upright
and go about our business,
which is in itself
another miracle.

Charyl K. Zehfus

THINGS THAT SKEW AND CANT, HAVE YET THEIR MUSIC IN THE STARS

No matter how we arrange
our lives, the fact is
things change.

Water rushes through the net,
the fist opens out empty,
there is nothing there to interpret.

Take a walk, and eat
the peaches that are growing wild,
and talk to the people in the street.

The man whose beard is long
   with voyage,
will show you in the palm of his hand
time's relentless ravage.

The angel does not sing on distant hill,
all looking overlooks the intrinsic,
the search for answers invites the peril.

All things that skew and cant,
have yet their music in the stars;
so move with consonance
among the haphazard nature of things,
and celebrate life's differences.

Take bird-chatter for a bride,
let the sea anoint the soul
and help to give it stride.
In the cathedral of the sky
full of the triumphal note of the living,
move like water,
many-mirrored and wise.

S. RAMNATH

THE BEGINNING
OF A BEGINNING

The past is but the beginning
of a beginning,
and all that is and has been
is but the twilight of the dawn.

H. G. WELLS

THIS IS OUR LORD'S WORLD

Time is all too brief,
Words spoken to one another, precious.
With visions of youth still fresh,
We grow toward adulthood with grace,

But we often stumble on that path,
Regretting what was said,
what wrong we may have caused.

This is our Lord's world.
We must treat it kindly
And believe in each other.

Time is all too brief.
Let us make these moments
Gentle . . . today.

JUDITH A. LINDBERG

A BETTER ME

The me I wish that I could be
Would never harm a soul,
Could never speak in angry tones,
Or have a selfish goal,
And no more wrong or harmful deeds
I'd ever want to do,
If this perfect ideal me
Could be a picture true.
The me I wish I could become
Will never really be,
But simply wanting such a thing
Will make a better me.

HILDA SANDERSON

SILENCE

Sometimes we forget the blessing
   of silence.
Sometimes the wind is poem enough,
the way a mountain hunches, the play
of sun across ocean in the space
   of a day.
Sometimes moss is a stanza, the orange
   of lichen
will stand in for a sonnet on a day
   like that.

RICHARD BEBAN

A PROVERB

No act of kindness,
   however small,
   is ever wasted.

AUTHOR UNKNOWN

KINDNESS

It is the history of our kindnesses
that alone makes this world tolerable.
If it were not for that, for the effect of
kind words, kind looks, kind letters . . .
I should be inclined to think our life
a practical jest in the worst possible spirit.

ROBERT LOUIS STEVENSON

TESTAMENT

Life is an open book,
A page turned every day,
We alone determine
What the story is to say.

Some are tales of triumph,
Others wrought with woe.
All have the same beginning—
The end we do not know.

Be the novel great or small,
The paper is the same.
Its content is the measure
Not the cover or the name.

Choose your message wisely,
Seek justice over wealth;
A classic for the ages—
Not dust upon the shelf.

When comes the final chapter,
And the pen is laid to rest,
May God in final judgment say—
We tried to write our best.

C. DAVID HAY

LEISURE

What is life if, full of care,
We have no time to stand and stare.

No time to stand beneath the boughs
And stare as long as sheep or cows.

No time to see, when woods we pass,
Where squirrels hide their nuts in grass.

No time to see, in broad daylight,
Streams full of stars, like stars at night.

No time to turn at Beauty's glance,
And watch her feet, how they can dance.

No time to wait till her mouth can
Enrich that smile her eyes began.

A poor life this if, full of care,
We have no time to stand and stare.

WILLIAM HENRY DAVIES

MY SYMPHONY
(ADAPTED)

Dear God,
Help me
To live content with small means,
to seek elegance rather than luxury,
and refinement rather than fashion,
to be worthy, not respectable, and
    wealthy, not rich,
to study hard, think quietly, talk gently,
    act frankly,
to listen to stars and birds, babes and
    sages, with open heart,
to bear all cheerfully,
do all bravely,
await occasions,
hurry never—
in a word, to let the spiritual, unbidden
    and unconscious,
grow up through the common.
This is to be my symphony.
Amen.

WILLIAM ELLERY CHANNING

OUR FOUNDATION

What we are today
   comes from
   our thoughts of yesterday,
   and our present thoughts
   build our life
   of tomorrow:

Our life is the creation of our mind.

THE BUDDHA

INHERITANCE

Often times the needy
Leave their children more
Than the ones with riches
Who were never poor.

Ones with wealth unending
May never understand
That to leave a child compassion
Is better than their land.

JOAN STEPHEN

BEATITUDES FOR FRIENDS
OF THE AGED

Blessed are they who understand my
faltering steps and palsied hand;

Blessed are they who know that my ears
today must strain to catch the things
they say.

Blessed are they who seem to know that
my eyes are dim and my wits are slow.

Blessed are they who looked away when
my coffee spilled at table today.

Blessed are they with a cheery smile
who stop to chat for a little while.

Blessed are they who never say "You've
told that story twice today."

Blessed are they who know the ways to
bring back memories of yesterdays.

Blessed are they who make it known
that I'm loved, respected and not alone.

Blessed are they who ease the days on
my journey Home in loving ways.

ESTHER M. WALKER

THE COMPLIMENT

I want to suggest a new Beatitude: "Blessed are the sincere who pay compliments."

For I have just had a compliment, and it has changed my day.

I was irritated. Tired. Discouraged. Nothing seemed much use. Now suddenly all this is changed.

I feel a spurt of enthusiasm, of energy and joy. I am filled with hope. I like the whole world better, and myself, and even you.

Lord, bless the person who did this for me.

He probably hasn't the faintest idea how his few words affected me. But wherever he is, whatever he's doing, bless him. Let him too feel this sense of fulfillment, this recharge of fire and faith and joy.

Thank you, God, for this simple miracle so available to all of us. And that we don't have to be saints to employ its power.

Remind me to use it more often to heal and lift and fortify others' lives: a compliment!

MARJORIE HOLMES

EARTH MOTHER

Earth mother, star mother
You who are called by
    a thousand names,
May all remember
    we are cells in your body
    and dance together.
You are the grain
    and the loaf
That sustains us each day,
And as you are patient
    with our struggles to learn
So shall we be patient
    with ourselves and each other
We are radiant light
    and scared dark
    —the balance—
You are the embrace that heartens
and the freedom beyond fear.
Within you we are born
    we grow, live, and die—

You bring us around the circle
     to rebirth,
Within us you dance
Forever.

STARHAWK

TIME

Time is
Too slow for those who Wait,
Too swift for those who Fear,
Too long for those who Grieve,
Too short for those who Rejoice;
   But for those who Love
     Time is not.

HENRY VAN DYKE
(1852–1933)

NIGHTFALL

PART FOUR

DREAMS

Dear God,

We give thanks for the darkness of the night where lies the world of dreams. Guide us closer to our dreams so that we may be nourished by them. Give us good dreams and memory of them so that we may carry their poetry and mystery into our daily lives.

Grant us deep and restful sleep that we may wake refreshed with strength enough to renew a world grown tired.

We give thanks for the inspiration of stars, the dignity of the moon and the lullabies of crickets and frogs.

Let us restore the night and reclaim it as a sanctuary of peace, where silence shall be music to our hearts and darkness shall throw light upon our souls.

Good night.

Sweet dreams.

Amen.

 LEUNIG

PREPARATION FOR PRAYER

Feet,
still, still now, upon the floor,
no need to hurry.

Hands,
lie quietly at rest,
no task to do just now.

Body,
relax in peace, serene;
now calmly rest.

Mind,
let go the scurrying,
let thought be still, so still.

Soul,
in silence vast as space,
reach, yearning, loving, unto God.

ELIZABETH SEARLE LAMB

COUNT THAT DAY LOST

If you sit down at set of sun
And count the acts that you have done,
  And, counting, find
One self-denying deed, one word
That eased the heart of him who heard,
  One glance most kind
That fell like sunshine where it went—
Then you may count that day well spent.

But if, through all the livelong day,
You've cheered no heart, by yea or nay—
  If, through it all
You've nothing done that you can trace
That brought the sunshine to one face—
  No act most small
That helped some soul and nothing cost—
Then count that day as worse than lost.

GEORGE ELIOT

THAT I MIGHT HEAR

Oh, holy night
fill with silence
that I might hear
that which is not spoken
by human voices.

SHARON ANN REICH-GRAY

PARADIGM FOR PRAYER

Daylight departs
darkness descends.
Sound surrenders,
silence surrounds.
Chatter concludes,
whispers widen.
Discord departs,
accord arrives.
Conflict ceases,
peace progresses.
Struggle slackens,
assent abides.
Details dissolve,
evening prayers.

SUSAN J. ERICKSON

LAST NIGHT, TONIGHT

Last night I dreamt
I walked across a stream
on a bridge made of flowers.
Chains of daisies arched
bank to bank
and I stepped out on petals
soft as flour,
hoping they would be
strong as flooring.

When I reached the far side I woke,
knowing You'd held my weight
as I walked over the border
between yesterday and tomorrow.

You carried me last night.
I trust You with tonight.

Evelyn Bence

STARRY FIELD

I was sunk into darkness
  and you lifted me to Light.
The ground was pulled from under me.
  You picked me up
  and set me again in your starry field.
I was weary. My eyes closed.
  You opened them
  and made me look.
My ears heard only laughter,
noise, and confusion.
  You sang a simple song,
  for the infant unable
  to make known its smallest need
    and said:
        "Let us begin."

I am beginning again.

JULIA OLDER

RELATIVITY

As you sleep, the moon
pours itself into your palms
as if they were holes to be filled,
as if the night blue veins
that run inside your wrists
were rivers to the dark interior

galaxy where your moon floats,
waxing and waning in the cage
of your ribs, shining
on the organs gravity has hung
around your heart.

And as you sleep the sun,
whose unsteady pulse beats
in a different cage, counts
neither your slow breaths
nor its own.

PENNY HARTER

RENEWAL

Lord, unwrinkle my tired soul
    unsnarl my garbled thoughts and words
    unwind my gnarled nerves
    and let me relax in Thee.

MARIAN WRIGHT EDELMAN

LET SLEEP COME

Now is the time to light the vesper
    candles of the soul
for their flame shall illuminate this
    sacred place.
Now is the time to rest in the indigo
    blue arms of the earth
for the earth shall support and
    embrace you.
Now is the time to dry the tears of
    the day
for the Spirit shall comfort and
    console you.
Now is the time to offer thanks for the
    blessings of this day
for the Spirit shall receive and honor
    your graciousness.
Now is the time to hear the lullaby of
    wind over the land
for you shall be rocked in the soothing
    comfort of its rhythm.
Now is the time to close your eyes and
    let sleep come
for the Spirit shall keep tender vigil
    through the night.

SUSAN J. ERICKSON

BLESSED WITH SIMPLICITY

A long and useful night alone
to relax, sit back, and write a poem.
Puttering around in my bare feet,
with peace and quiet a special treat.
I know that others may have more
  than me
but I feel blessed with simplicity.

PEGGY WARD

ON GOING TO BED

As my head rests on my pillow
Let my soul rest in your mercy.

As my limbs relax on my mattress,
Let my soul relax in your peace.

As my body finds warmth beneath the
   blankets,
Let my soul find warmth in your love.

As my mind is filled with dreams,
Let my soul be filled with visions of
   heaven.

JOHANN FREYLINGHAUSEN
(1670–1739)

TWILIGHT

Before I fall behind
the veil of sleep,
let my prayers be heard
by the stars and held
heaven-high
on their wings of light.
And if my soul surrenders
its flesh this night,
let my body return
to earth's dark womb,
but send my soul to dance
among the prayers
that hold the night.

JOEY GARCIA

AFTER THE TURBULENCE OF
THE DAY

After the turbulence of the day,
thank you for sending the peacefulness
  of the night.
How blessed the peace of the night,
so still
that the very tones
of mountain and skyscraper
lose their jutty, harsh aspect
and bathe in thrilling stillness.

Let us not ruminate upon
the disagreeable scenes of the day.
Let us not rehearse
injustices,
bitter, hard words,
coarse actions.

Mindful, Father,
of your infinite patience with us,
your infinite goodness,
we ask you to help us
never to harbor a single drop
of hatred, or resentment,
or bitterness
against anyone.

Fill us
with your limitless mercy.

G. Helder Camara

WELCOME SILENCE

Dear God in Heaven,
   All day I wrestle,
   struggle with the constant noise
   barraged from all extremes;
   but now I nestle,
   curled within night silence
   that lets me hear You whispering in
     my dreams.

GAIL McCOIG BLANTON

IN CLOSING

As I turn off the light
And prepare for the night
I thank you, Lord, for the gift
      of today
For the comfortable bed
      on which I lay.
I thank you, Lord, for the
      strength to be
Open to those who have needed me.
In peaceful slumber I shall
      know no fear
For you, my Saviour, are
      always near.
Amen.

BEATRICE O'BRIEN

IN SILENCE

The moon
sends ripples of light
into the darkness
of the pond,
the shadows
dappled
by drifting clouds;
so does faith
send its shaft
of hope and peace
into consciousness
as I drift
into the darkness
of sleep.

ELIZABETH SEARLE LAMB

EVENING PRAYER

Dear Lord,
I sense you listen and see.
I cannot sleep
until we speak.
Forgive me the mistakes I've made,
the wrong deeds done this day.
Love me most
when I love myself least.

JACQUELINE SEEWALD

A PARENT'S PRAYER

Oh, misty moon, with star beside it;
In a heaven gray and silent—
Bring home my child from afar;
This my wish upon a star.
Hear my plea through darkened night
Always keep my child in sight.

JOAN STEPHEN

A MOTHER'S BEDTIME PRAYER

This day is finally over!
I thought it would never end.
The children drove me crazy;
I quarreled with my friend.

I burned the meat at supper
When I took a salesman's call;
I snapped my husband's head off
For no good reason at all.

I'm thankful this day has ended—
Forgive me for going astray;
Lord, help me to face tomorrow
And stay close beside me all day.

Amen.

DORIS L. MUELLER

PRIORITIES

From the top of the antique armoire
high above my bed
the television blares,
a nightly tower of babble;
but tonight its ritual is canceled.
I have willed to take control,
for my prayers have become as
remote and cold as this plastic wand in
   my hand.
The shocking truth of parenthood
struck me today as my toddler
stood so pitifully weeping
inconsolable
in supplication lifting up his little
   hands—
not to me, I must confess,
but to a silent TV set no one had yet
   turned on.
Father, I lift my arms, crying up to you;
May a prayer lull me to sleep at night
and wake me to a balanced day.

GAIL MCCOIG BLANTON

A PETITION FOR THE SLEEPLESS

I kneel before Your throne tonight, My Lord,
on a cushion of contentment
and fully expect a night of restful sleep.
If it please You, Majesty,
I ask a further favor:
That You sustain and solace
those who cannot sleep tonight.
    Your subjects who:

Are old and wakeful	Work the night shifts
Are worried for a missing child	Groan in pain
Are haunted by their conscience	Study for exams
Keep a sickbedvigil	Mourn a loved one lost
Are cold, hungry, imprisoned	Stumble in the wild woods

and so are unable to sleep like I.
Dispatch swift-flying couriers to help
    them through the night.
    I humbly thank You, My Lord, Your
    Grace.

GAIL McCOIG BLANTON

A NIGHTTIME BLESSING

Bless those who breathe
In the stardust
Of night.

Bless those who rise
At the breaking
Of light.

Let us shine.
Let us shine.
Let us shine.

Peter Markus

COUPLE

Dear Lord,
As we kneel together by our bed
Let us be intimate with You
as we are with one another
   love anticipating love
   touch exhilarating touch
   faith trusting in faithfulness
   mindful of partaking of wonder
   rejoicing in the contentment
    of one flesh,
    one Lord, one Spirit.

GAIL McCOIG BLANTON

SINGLE

Like crystal beads spilled on a
  jeweler's cloth
the stars are set before me through
  the skylight,
an engaging sight;
yet no one has chosen me
to string along.
Clasp me, Lord,
against this loneliness;
kiss me with sweet dreams.
Give me patience to believe
that my star
is waiting in Your wings.

GAIL McCOIG BLANTON

SURRENDER TO THE UNKNOWN

Sleep is a surrender
to unknowing
A turning in to mystery
An abandonment to dreams undisclosed
Much like
My yielding to Your knowing
A turning toward the mystic
When I fold back the sheets
I am folding all my being
into Yours
And so am beginning to Be, anew;
Morning is in Your hands.

GAIL MCCOIG BLANTON

THE ROARING WATERFALL

The roaring waterfall
is the Buddha's golden mouth.
The mountains in the distance
are his pure luminous body.
How many thousands of poems
have flowed through me tonight!
And tomorrow I won't be able
to repeat even one word.

Su Tung-P'o
(1036–1101)

A SUMMER NIGHT'S PRAYER
(Evensong)

The summer day unfolds its wings
  Like time flying.
All day, bright light sings like a swan,
  Dying.

Light floats down from the sky, light
  As a feather.
It drifts toward night
  And a change of weather.

The sun sets suddenly, burning
  Bridges, the blaze rising higher
And higher over the earth's methodical
    turning.
  Night puts out the fire.

All things cool and harden, after being
    singed.
  Day gives way to night.
The song the white swan sang,
  Day sings tonight.

In the silence that ensues, all things
   Close up; night
Snuggles its head in its protective wings
   All night.

The living room lights blink on, then off.
   People and pets all sleep.
Time that flew, now sinks
   Into the laky deep.

All sleep.

KELLY CHERRY

STAR WISH

I saw a shooting star
As it blazed across the night
And marveled at the beauty
Of such a fleeting sight.

For one brief fiery instant
It flamed for all to see,
Then faded into darkness—
A brilliant memory.

Countless lights in endless space,
The splendor of the skies—
A star is always brightest
Just before it dies.

God grant me such a blessing
That peers may someday say—
I had my shining moment
As I passed this way.

C. DAVID HAY

PLACE ME IN A ROCKETSHIP

Place me in a rocketship
Streaking in a silent sweep
Across the swirl of star-filled sky,
And I will seed the night with prayer.

YAACOR DAVID SHULMAN

PLEASE GIVE ME A NIGHT

Please give me a night
Whose great, shining wings
Lift me above the twinkling houses;
Please help me greet the night
As a dark messenger at the door,
And ride with him on the empty road
to the field where the table is set with
    books
And the laurels gently quiver,
Until I return, as the road grows light,
And sneak into the waking house.

Please help me stride through sleeping
    towns,
Where houses seem abandoned in the
    streetlights' glow,
Where only the trees are still awake,
And the stars are singing to me, "Join us";
And may I take a needle from my sleeve
And weave the stars and trees with words,
And may I weave with threads of night
The caftan which I don at dawn.
Please help me pour the indigo sky
Upon my hands, and wipe the
    sparkling stars across my eyes.

Please help me walk the road which
    leads from night
To the hill where trees appear with
    purple branches
And the people hurry from their homes,
While I know that I have worn the suit
    of night
And danced, as the world was muted.

Yaacor David Shulman

NIGHT

Night binds love with dreams.
The window open, wind
silent, no longer the angry voice
of day and sand and dust
in children's eyes.

The household sleeps.
Ninja turtles clutched in moist fists,
the wheezy breath of the Ancient One
down the hall.
A thousand crickets on the hill.

JORDAN CLARY

THE NIGHT SKY

When something taps your window
in the dark—a large moth
beating its pale wings,
or a pungent branch of lilac
scraping in the wind—
you wake to the night sky
pouring in upon you.

You have been waiting
all your life for this,
open as a harp.

And when a bird cries out
from the depths of the lilac
where it has slept every night
undisturbed, you understand
that it too has opened
to a shining that sings.

PENNY HARTER

LULLABY OF PROMISE

Soothe me with a lullaby of promise;
Rock me, singing certainties of rest:
guarded with a strong and valiant angel,
cradled in Your love and sweetly blessed,
pillowed in a beam of Heaven's light,
covered by soft mercy through the night.

GAIL MCCOIG BLANTON

EVENING'S PROMISE

I pray
  Softly
In the silent darkness,
Watching earth
Slip into the shadows of heaven
As starlit embers
  Like guideposts
Flicker to welcome us home.

JANIE BOWMAN

Morning

PART FIVE

- - - - - -

SONNET TO MORNING

Let me unwrap the gift of this new day
And view its contents as an innocent
    child
Accepts the world: with eyes that see
    the way
To sun beyond dark clouds, where
    skies are mild;
With voice that lifts in prayer, as birds
    praise dawn;
With hands that touch each miracle, in
    awe
Of budding leaves or flowers on a lawn
Or furry friends with hoof and horn
    and paw.
Lead me along a path where I will find
In all the precious hours that stretch
    before,
The chance to help, to listen, to be kind;
To heal the wounds that make the
    world heartsore.
Oh, let me fill each second so that I
May greet the day with an appreciative
    eye.

SHEILA FORSYTH

GIVE MY SOUL A HEAVENLY HUSH

Let me tarry as I go;
if not my feet, my heart be slow.
As I run from rush to rush
give my soul a heavenly hush—
That I may touch instead of shove,
That I may see those needing love.
In passing may I leave a glow;
of kindly words that help peace grow.

GAIL MCCOIG BLANTON

A LEBANESE PRAYER

O God, Creator of Light:
at the rising
of your sun this morning,
let the greatest of all light,
    your love,
rise like the sun within our hearts.
Amen.

ARMENIAN APOSTOLIC CHURCH

THE NUN'S TWENTY-THIRD PSALM

The Lord is my pace-setter, I shall not
   rush.
He makes me stop and rest for quiet
   intervals;
He provides me with images of stillness,
      which restore my serenity.
He leads me in ways of efficiency
      through calmness of mind.
And His guidance is peace.
Even though I have a great many
      things to accomplish each day,
I will not fret, for His presence is here.
His timelessness, his all-importance
      will keep me in balance.
He prepares refreshment and renewal
      in the midst of my activity
By anointing my mind with His oils of
      tranquillity.

ALL SAINTS CONVENT
CANTONVILLE, MARYLAND

ONE TIME, I ENTERED HEAVEN

it was on a quiet morn
when the world slept deeply
and the spirits swirled like water

imagine
skipping on clouds
leaping from star to star

it was the music, you see
it was the notes the angels
had carefully fastened to the breeze

sometimes
I gather them like stardust
sometimes
in between the greed and cry of the
    wolf
when the moon pauses
when the earth catches its awesome
    breath

I can hear the bells peal
I can feel the face of God
mirrored in the dips and dives of a
   dove

sometimes
when I listen

as the angels embrace
the crystal dewy dawn

MIKE MAGGIO

MORNING PRAYER

When little things would irk me,
  and I grow
Impatient with my dear one,
  make me know
How in a moment joy can take its flight
And happiness be quenched in
  endless night.
Keep this thought with me all the
  livelong day
That I may guard the harsh words
  I might say
When I would fret and grumble,
  fiery hot
At trifles that tomorrow are forgot—
Let me remember, Lord, how it
  would be
If these, my loved ones, were not here
  with me.

ELLA WHEELER WILCOX

LOOKING OUT THE HOSPITAL WINDOW

How can we see the night-rinsed rays
of the sun painting pre-dawn sky
and still think with colorless minds
that this is an ordinary day?

As the sun opens up the sky
with a heartfelt wash of cobalt blue
the box mind says, "I've seen this hue
before, about 12,000 times."

But when we've tasted head-on ruin
or some catastrophe has shocked
the mind to silence, then we stop
and know, "My God! This dawn is new."

KATHY CONDE

LIVING PAGES

Let me leave margins of silence
around the activities of day,
letting You write down there
whatever it is You would say.

Then looking backward, I find,
no matter how much I revise,
it is in Your footnotes
that the heart of my life lies.

ELIZABETH SEARLE LAMB

WITH CLEARER EYE

If only I could see today,
 In everyone that comes my way,
A child of God, though dimly drawn,
 Then no one, Lord, would be a pawn
To use in any scheme of mine,
 However grand, or warped design . . .

If only, passing on the street,
In every stranger I may meet . . .
 The businessman who rushes by,
 The homeless one, with downcast eye,
 The mother with the child in tow,
 The rowdy kids that laughing go,
 The actress with her haughty look,
 The student with his bag and book . . .

A child of Thine, I could discern,
 The heart in me, oh Lord, would burn
To look on each with kind regard,
 And not with looks indifferent, hard.
In each, if only I might see
 The essence of humanity
And godliness, though blurred the grace;
 For all that breathe reflect God's face.

Oh, let me see with clearer eye—
A child of God just walked on by.

WILLIAM DEERFIELD

A MORNING MEDITATION

Today let me touch the Earth
with gentle hands
and build anew.

Tomorrow let me remember
that all that I have built
belongs to Earth alone.

And always
let me ask for no other blessing
than the one that God has already
    given me:
To Be.

DANIEL ROSELLE

MORNING SILENCE

Aroused by light that softly
permeates my mind,
I sit up secretly to offer You my prayer.
Words that tremble in the air,
thoughts said in the mind in silence,
reach the regions where You hear.
As I breathe in, as I breathe out,
I find the place where You are near,
smiling in my silence.

WAVE CARBERRY

SUNRISE IN YOUR HEART

May the Great Mystery make
sunrise in your heart.

S<small>IOUX</small> I<small>NDIAN</small> <small>SAYING</small>

AUTOGRAPH

God wrote His autograph
Upon the sky last night,
In stars I never saw
A signature as bright.

With the dawn again
For watchers to behold—
He wrote His name in sunlight,
An autograph of gold.

Marion Schoeberlein

LET YOUR LIGHT DAWN
IN OUR MINDS

O God, let fear die and conviction be
     born in our lives.
Let Your light dawn in our minds as
     the day dawns on the earth.
Let us not be so busy hurrying into the
     future and worrying about the
     past that we lose today—the only
     one we have.
God, help us do what we know
     we have to do today, and leave
     tomorrow to You.

MARIAN WRIGHT EDELMAN

MIRACLE OF THE LIGHT

Miracle of the light: the shadow is born,
it strikes in silence against the mountains,
tumbles weightlessly to the ground,
keeping the delicate grasses awake.
The eucalyptus trees leave upon the earth
the trembling bark of their lengthened
silhouette, over which fly cold
birds that do not sing.
A slighter and simpler shadow,
born from your legs, comes forward
to announce the ultimate, the purest
miracle of the light: you against the dawn.

ÁNGEL GONZÁLEZ
*Astonishing World: The Selected Poems
 of Ángel González, 1956–1986*
TRANSLATED FROM SPANISH BY
 STEVEN FORD BROWN AND
 GUTIERREZ REVUELTA

MORNING RUSH

Let me bustle gently, Lord.
Let me carefully careen,
and not disrupt my family,
around, below, between.
Let me be efficient, yes,
but not a mad machine.

Let me panic quietly
when I see the clock's caprice,
and send them off with tender touch
that wipes away the hustle grease.
Let me bustle gently, Lord;
Let me always keep Your peace.

GAIL McCOIG BLANTON

MORNING SONG

Every morning when you rise
Sing some merry song;
The one that is the cheeriest
And brightens up the dawn.
Make a smile that's happy
With eyes that ever gleam
And always keep your spirit
Prepared for every dream.

JOAN STEPHEN

A PRAYER FOR PERMEABILITY

Lord, infuse me with love, this day
as tea diffuses its flavor in water,
as tarragon lends its essence to vinegar,
as mint releases its sweetness in jelly,
as woodruff imparts its fragrance to wine,
as sunlight glazes winter clouds,
Lord, infuse me with your light.

BARBARA CROOKER

A PRAYER AT DAWN

Dear God of Light,
Dawn has arrived
Painting a rainbow of many colors
Against an opening sky.

Hold me close
As day breaks away from darkness
And my footsteps falter.
Help me to seek wisdom and under-
standing,
To return deeds of kindness
And comfort a small child.

I am only a breath in time
Riding with the sun.
Remind me, please,
To walk gently
Into this new light.

JANIE BOWMAN

ALWAYS NEAR

As the dawn
mists
over the horizon

and the sun
closes
its evening shade,

it's with such
certainty
I know

You are always near.

JUNE COTNER GRAVES

The following are upcoming anthologies for which I will continue to seek submissions:

Prayers of the Universe: Prayers and Poems to Honor the Human Values That Unite Us All. The overriding theme is unity in diversity (the commonality of all). Other themes are love (for humankind), peace, forgiveness, compassion, spirituality, nature and the environment, our children, friends and family, community and worldly concerns, wonder and appreciation, praise and celebration, tolerance, hope for the future, and inspiration.

Family Celebrations: Prayers and Poems for All Occasions.

Animal Blessings: Prayers and Poems to Honor the Creatures with Whom We Share the Earth. I particularly like poems that share the perspective of what we can learn from animals.

Blessed with Simplicity: Poems and Gentle Thoughts for Living in Harmony with the Universe. I am seeking poems that address the theme of slowing down and scaling back to enjoy a more simple life.

Whatever Is—Is Best: Prayers and Poems for Accepting Loss and Overcoming Hardship.

Prayers of Loss: Prayers and Poems on Illness, Death, Grieving, and Healing.

The Peaceful Heart: An Inspirational Treasury of Spiritual Poetry.

Our Ride Among the Stars: Prayers and Poems to Celebrate the Wonder of Life (a book for children).

If you'd like to submit something for a future book, typed copies are always appreciated (with your name, address, and phone number at the top of each page). If you include a self-addressed, stamped envelope, you'll eventually receive a reply. I hope to hear from you!

June Cotner
P.O. Box 2765
Poulsbo, WA 98370

INDEX OF AUTHORS

PERMISSIONS AND ACKNOWLEDGMENTS

Grateful acknowledgment is made to the authors and publishers for the use of the following material. Every effort has been made to contact original sources. If notified, the publisher will be pleased to rectify an omission in future editions.

Bantam Books for "Illumination" from *Hearts that We Broke Long Ago* by Merle Shain, copyright © 1983 by Merle Shain. Reprinted by permission of Bantam Books, a division of Bantam Doubleday Dell Publishing Group, Inc.

Ellen Bass for "The Thing Is."

Beacon Press for "Let Your Light Dawn in Our Minds," "Lord, Help Me," "Renewal," and "The Nun's Twenty-third Psalm" from *Guide My Feet* by Marian Wright Edelman, copyright © 1995 by Marian Wright Edelman. Reprinted by permission of Beacon Press, Boston.

Richard Beban for "Silence."

Evelyn Bence for "Last Night, Tonight."

Gail McCoig Blanton for "A Petition for

Corrine DeWinter for "Somehow."

Kris Ediger for "Heart of My Heart."

Jan Edwards for "The Voice Within" and "A Private Place."

Susan J. Erickson for "Paradigm for Prayer" and "Let Sleep Come."

Sheila Forsyth for "Sonnet to Morning."

Joey Garcia for "Twilight."

Theresa Mary Grass for "Daily Prayer" and "Let Me Be a Light."

June Cotner Graves for "Always Near."

Maryanne Hannan for "Epiphany."

HarperCollins for "Earth Mother" from *Earth Prayers* by Elizabeth Roberts and Elias Amidon. Copyright © 1991 by HarperCollins. Reprinted with permission from HarperCollins.

HarperCollins*Religious* for "Dreams" from *A Common Prayer* by Michael Leunig. Copyright © 1990 by Michael Leunig. Used with permission of Harper Collins*Religious*, Melbourne, Australia.

Penny Harter for "Relativity" and "The Night Sky."

Harvard University Press for "Hope" reprinted by permission of the publish-

Mike Maggio for "One Time, I Entered Heaven."

Peter Markus for "A Nighttime Blessing."

Milkweed Editions for "Miracle of the Light" from *Astonishing World: The Selected Poems of Ángel González, 1956–1986*, translated from the Spanish by Steven Ford Brown and Gutierrez Revuelta and edited by Steven Ford Brown (Milkweed Editions, 1993). English language translation by Steven Ford Brown and Gutierrez Revuelta. Reprinted with permission from Milkweed Editions.

Monica Miller for "These I Wish."

Doris L. Mueller for "A Mother's Bedtime Prayer."

Joan Noëldechen for "The Inner Flame."

Beatrice O'Brien for "In Closing."

Julia Older for "Starry Field."

S. Ramnath for "Things That Skew and Cant, Have Yet Their Music in the Stars."

Sharon Ann Reich-Gray for "That I Might Hear."

Riverhead Books for "I Live My Life in Widening Circles" and "You See, I Want a Lot" by Rainer Maria Rilke. Reprinted

by Tertius Van Dyke.

Joan Stephen for "A Parent's Prayer," "Inheritance," "Morning Song," "Psalm of Tranquility," "The Candle," "The Gift," and "Trust Him."

Mary A. Summerline for "The Land of Eternal Love."

Gale Swiontkowski for "Soul-Home."

Unity Press for "In Silence," "Living Pages," and "Preparation for Prayer" from *Today and Every Day* by Elizabeth Searle Lamb. Copyright © 1970 by Unity School of Christianity. Reprinted by permission of Unity Books, 1901 NW Blue Parkway, Unity Village, MO 64065.

Peggy Ward for "Blessed with Simplicity."

Joanna M. Weston for "To Be Still."

Charyl K. Zehfus for "A Miracle."

Look for these *HarperLargePrint books* at your local bookstore

HarperLargePrint Classics
Published in deluxe paperback editions in
easy-to-read 16-point type

Pride and Prejudice, Jane Austen
A Tale of Two Cities, Charles Dickens
The Adventures of Sherlock Holmes, Sir Arthur Conan Doyle
This Side of Paradise, F. Scott Fitzgerald
A Room with a View, E.M. Forster
To Kill a Mockingbird, Harper Lee

Also available from HarperLargePrint
Bedside Prayers, June Cotner
Calder Pride, Janet Dailey
How to Get What You Want and Want What You Have,
John Gray, Ph.D.
Mars and Venus Starting Over, John Gray, Ph.D.
The Anti-Aging Zone, Barry Sears, Ph.D.
Beauty Fades, Dumb is Forever, Judy Sheindlin
A God in Ruins, Leon Uris
Little Altars Everywhere, Rebecca Wells
Worst Fears Realized, Stuart Woods

HarperLargePrint books are available
at your local bookstore, or call 1-800-331-3761, or write:
HarperLargePrint
10 East 53rd Street, New York, New York, 10022
www.harpercollins.com